I Call My Sugar, Candie

Youssef Khalim

Copyright © 2013 Youssef Khalim

All rights reserved.

ISBN: 978-0-9787798-8-7
ISBN-13: 978-0978779887

DEDICATION

To: Lori (The real or ideal soul mate: inspiration)

Tonya Tracy Khalim and

Runako Soyini Khalim, (my most beloved daughters)

Mother and Grandmother and Great-grandmother, (my most beloved maternal biological ancestors, and spiritual antecedents)

M. A. Garvey (one of my 7 M's: my role models)

Youssef Khalim II; III (my most beloved sons)

Father and Grandfather and Great-grandfather, (my most beloved paternal biological ancestors, and spiritual antecedents)

To: The Forerunners and Reincarnation sources (beloved bio- logical ancestors and spiritual antecedents), and

The Almighty (our Spiritual Father), from whence we come.

CONTENTS

	Acknowledgments	i
1	Introduction	1
2	Upon This Rock	Pg 2
3	I Should Get to Know You?	Pg 3
4	Candie	Pg 4
5	I Love You	Pg 5
6	I Think About You Once Each Day	Pg 6
7	I Simply Have to See You!	Pg 7
8	You Want to Play?	Pg 8
9	Do You Like It?	Pg 9
10	I Call My Sugar, Candie	Pg 11
11	What I Love About You	Pg 12
12	Why Not?	Pg 13
13	The Second Time	Pg 14
14	Did You Ever Feel Like A Lollipop?	Pg 15
15	Candie is Sweet	Pg 16
16	I Love the Sweet Taste of You	Pg 17
17	Did You Go To The Street Party?	Pg 18
18	Know How	Pg 20
19	Your Presence is Here, My Lord	Pg 21
20	I Love You, Father	Pg 22

21	Praise, Honor, Love, and Glory	Pg 22
22	Which Reminds Me of You	Pg 24
23	Amazing to Behold!	Pg 25
24	I Love to See You	Pg 26
25	About the Author, and Other Books	Pg 27

ACKNOWLEDGMENTS

To: The Forerunners and Reincarnation sources (beloved bio- logical ancestors and spiritual antecedents), and

   The Almighty (our Spiritual Father), from whence we come.

1 INTRODUCTION

I Call My Sugar, Candie, is the last in a series of eight books by Youssef Khalim, begun in 2002. Four were inspired by ladies encountered over- seas. *Candie* is one of the four inspired by Americans.

In the Introduction, Khalim says: "I met Candie in Wicker Park, in Chicago, during the beautiful summer of 2005. She was sweet, and inspirational. So I started to write about her, about feelings, about life. The rest (as they say) is history!"

I Call My Sugar, Candie is cute, fun, and sweet! Needless to say, your collection of Khalim's works will be missing a key ingredient without *Candie*.

        Youssef Khalim
        2/3/2006

2 UPON THIS ROCK

Are you familiar with the saying,
"Upon *this rock* I will build my Church,
And the gates of hell shall not prevail against it?"

Well, it reminds me,
We will upgrade *it*, if that's ok.

Well, do you remember that saying?
OK. We'll talk about it.

We will build it upon *this rock*!
Do you know what I mean?

3 I SHOULD GET TO KNOW YOU?

OK, Candie,
You know how much
I love you,
And want you,
And need you,

So…,
Don't you think
I should get to know you?

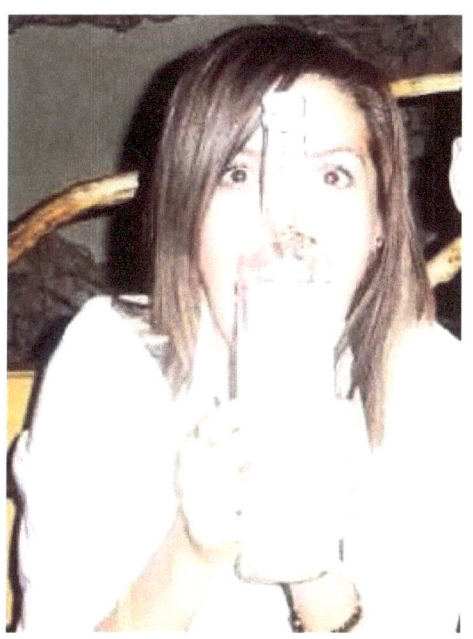

4 CANDIE

Candie,
I just love to
Kiss
Your beautiful, sexy,
Warm, sweet
Mouth,
To start!

5 I LOVE YOU

I love you,
I love you.
(Do you want some more?)

OK, sweetheart,
I love you, sweet Candie,
I love you.

6 I THINK ABOUT YOU ONCE EACH DAY

I think about you
Once each day,
I mean, I think of you,
All day long!

I love you, likewise,
Once each day.

I love you, sweetheart!
All day long!

7 I SIMPLY HAVE TO SEE YOU!

You looked so beautiful,
Lovely, radiant, and sexy,
When I last saw you!

Stimulating, and exciting!

I love seeing you
Because
You make my day!

Arouse me, and
Strengthen me!

So, now,
I simply have to see you,
Every day!

8 YOU WANT TO PLAY?

You are a
Very, very good model!

And you can

Play
Any role

You want to play
With me.

9 DO YOU LIKE IT?

Do you like to hear me say,
"I love you?"

Do you want a love
That makes your heart and face smile,
And leaves your body radiant, glowing?

Do you like it,
When I give you what you want?

Do you want my love to make you happy,
Expand your imagination,
Cosmically?

Then,
Please you,
Please you,
And please you?

Do you like it?

10 I CALL MY SUGAR, CANDIE

Yes, I call my Sugar, Candie.
Yes, I'm sweet on Candie,
'Cause Candie's sweet.

I mean,
She's delicious-sweet!
& sexy, gorgeous!

Yes, I call my Sugar, Candie,
'Cause,
Candie is…

Sweet!

11 WHAT I LOVE ABOUT YOU

I love your beautiful, sexy mouth,
Your eyes & smile,
Your conversation(s),
Your beautiful face,
Your sexy, curvy chest, & hips, &
Your walk;
Your industrious, enterprising, & intelligent spirit,
Your inspiration,
The exciting & stimulating thought of you,
Your conversation(s),
(Oh, I said that.)
The way you turn me on,
& your beautiful, sexy mouth!

12 WHY NOT?

Yes, I love you.
(How did you know that,
I mean, before I ever told you?)

It's very, very easy
To love you,
And be in-love with you

Because of your
Extremely attractive,
Radiant and charismatic personality-
And hot body!

And since I want you so,
And need you (more),

Why Not?

13 THE SECOND TIME

The second time I saw you,
I fell in-love with you…

Hmmmm.

Or, maybe it was the
First time!

14 DID YOU EVER FEEL LIKE A LOLLIPOP?

Did you ever feel like a lollipop,
Or a rainbow,
Or a rainbow colored lollipop?

Do you like orange-flavored sunrise(s), and sunset(s)?

Stood at the end of a rainbow?
Want to be my lollipop?

Have you ever studied man?
Are you the other half?

What day will you complete me,
So, I can experience sunrise and sunset – all at once,
And scale the tallest rainbow,
Know all about man – and wo-man, together,

And love you, taste you,
Consume you,

So we both are sweet?

15 CANDIE IS SWEET

Candie is sweet,
Beautiful, sexy, lovely,
Helpful,
Well, … everything,
& very, very sweet!

16 I LOVE THE SWEET TASTE OF YOU

Candie,
You are:
And look,
So delicious!
So sweet & sexy!

I have a taste for you, &

I love the scent of you,
To touch you,
Hold you,
Caress you
Kiss you,
And love the sweet, sweet taste
Of you forever!

17 DID YOU GO TO THE STREET PARTY?

Candie, sometimes I see you in my mind, just doing things:

Which reminds me, did you go to the Street Party, that was in the streets, right outside your business?

And did you see the band? WOW! They really jammed!

The speakers were blaring! The streets and sidewalks echoed the music and the beat!

The Band was high intensity, grooving! They had high energy!

People danced in the streets, and bounced to the music, even when they just passed by, walking down the streets or sidewalks.

Some folks stood around, swaying to that heavy beat and electric music.

Onlookers and passersby had joy written all across their faces. Did you see anybody who seemed unhappy at the Street Party?

I saw one man tossing and dribbling a basketball with a child, maybe his son.

One couple danced together. The man was showing off, turning, spinning, smiling, and egging the woman on!

Which reminds me: I pictured you there, your hips moving to the music, your feet beginning to move a little. How could your feet resist that beat?

I pictured us there together, holding hands. And then, we danced, just like the couple I saw.

Which reminds me: Do you like to stroll together, holding hands?

Do you like to dance?
Will you party with me?

Which reminds me: I see us together forever, holding hands, strolling together, Street Party, or no Street Party! I see your smile!

I see us making music,
Sweet, as sweet as Candie.
I see us dance!
I see *us* party!

18 KNOW HOW

OK, I need to find out more
About you.

How else can I
Know how
To
Love you,
And please you?

Desperately,
I need you!

Desperately,
I need to love you!

And desperately,
I need to please you!

I have a way,
To find out more.

Do you want to
Know how?

19 YOUR PRESENCE IS HERE, MY LORD

Candie, you know I practice yoga.
And you know I'm very spiritual.

This is one way I get spiritual energy to flow throughout my mind, body, and soul.

I think ...

Your presence is near, my Lord !
Your presence is near, my Lord!
Your presence is near, my Lord!
Your presence is near, my Lord!

Your presence is near, my Lord!
Your presence is near, my Lord!
Your presence is near, my Lord!
Your presence is *here,* my Lord!

All praise to God,
Amen.

20 I LOVE YOU, FATHER

Candie, this is another way I get spiritual energy to flow throughout my mind, body, and soul. *I think...*

> I love you (Father), with
> Love, faith, and trust
> Love, faith, and trust
> Love, faith, and trust
> Love, faith, and trust,
> With
> Love, faith, and trust
> Love, faith, and trust
> Love, faith, and trust
> Love, faith, and trust
>
> I love you (Father),
> OM.

21 PRAISE, HONOR, LOVE AND GLORY!

Candie, this is yet another way that I get spiritual energy to flow throughout my mind, body, and soul.

I give:

Praise, honor, love, and glory (to God)
Praise, honor, love, and glory
Praise, honor, love, and glory
Praise, honor, love, and glory

Praise, honor, love, and glory
Praise, honor, love, and glory
Praise, honor, love, and glory
Praise, honor, love, and glory

OM.

22 WHICH REMINDS ME OF YOU

Candie, the other night,
I was out, about 2:15 AM
Doing some Test Calls for our Telecommunications Network.

I was over on Fullerton, just east of Racine, by the Public Library parking lot.

I saw this couple,
Which reminded me of us.
I noticed the woman,
Who reminded me of you.

She was posing, showing off:
"I'm the most beautiful woman in the world:"
She showed, strutting around.

You look perfect: just like Candie! (I thought.)

But you know, the Bible says the woman was made from the rib of a man, probably the marrow.

No wonder you (woman) are sometimes perfect:
The first human clone!

Perfect like a flower,
Or a circle, curvy,
Beautiful, lovely, gorgeous,
Delicious:

Which reminds me of you!

23 AMAZING TO BEHOLD

You are fantastically beautiful,
Stunningly beautiful,
Lovely,
Sexy, gorgeous,
Wonderful, and
Amazing to behold!

24 I LOVE TO SEE YOU

I love to see you,
Hear your voice.

Baby, you are my
Love of choice.

Your curvy hips
Make my heart skip -
A beat
When you walk.

With you I soar;
You make my engine roar,

As long as clear bright skies are blue :
Candie, Darling, I will love you.

I love you, love you.
I'd love to see you today.

25 ABOUT THE AUTHOR, AND OTHER BOOKS

Youssef Khalim obtained Unity in yoga on about 7/20/80. He says, "We will recombine into one faith, Judaism, Christianity, and Islam." He has been able to "see" and experience some amazing information about USA presidents Jefferson, Lincoln, and Obama; and also Prophets Moses, Muhammad, and Solomon - in visions, lucid dreams, and in meditation. Khalim makes reincarnation (resurrection) central again in our western religions. He resides in the Chicagoland area. And he is the father of Tonya, Runako, and Noah. See his books on the following websites: http://amazon.com, http://lulu.com, and http://sunracommunications.com

 OTHER BOOKS

Youssef Khalim's books include *People Of The Future/Day; You Are Too Beautiful; I Love You Back; You Look So Good; The Resurrection Of Noah; Healing Begins With The Mind; Jubilee Worldwide; Lara, Forever; Tanisha Love; Galina, All About Love; Ekaterina, Hot and Lovely; Natalia, With Love; Svetlana, Angel Of Love; I Call My Sugar, Candie*; *Love of My Life;* and *The Second Coming!*

www.ingramcontent.com/pod-product-compliance
Lightning Source LLC
Chambersburg PA
CBHW042306150426

43197CB00001B/39